MW00653127

So Long Inner Critic
Hello Inner Champion

Tips to Master Your Mindset

Marcie Stern, MHA, RLC

Creator of the WAAMM™ Principle

i

Advance Praise for *So Long Inner Critic, Hello Inner Champion: 25 Tips to Master Your Mindset*

"If you deal with negativity or an inner critic, this book will teach you how to change your critic into a champion, and your negativity into positive progress. Marcie Stern shares practical advice you can use to improve your mindset for a successful life." *–Mark Sanborn, President of Sanborn And Associates Inc., Speaker and bestselling author of The Fred Factor*

"As an HR professional, Consultant and Coach, I have seen my share of individuals who have been hired because of their education, experience and skill-set but have found themselves stalled in their careers because of the critic within. They are hesitant to take charge of situations for fear that they might not really be the right person to do so, or they may decide to let a good idea fade because they are not sure they can stand up and sell the idea and themselves. We all have inner critics but some seem to be louder than others. The tips in this book can help tremendously to tame that inner critic and to get back on a path of success and professional growth. This book is easy to read and reinforces all the right behaviors and actions that can make a difference to one's personal and professional life." *–Donna de St. Aubin, Principal, St. Aubin Haggerty & Associates, Inc.*

"Marcie Stern has written the ultimate guide for anyone who wants to buckle down and get rid of an inner critic. In a gentle yet firm style, she encourages with constant opportunities for self-analysis and action steps. Dotted with very fitting quotes from the famous and non-famous, the book also cites real-life success stories from those who have mastered a new mindset. A special note should be made about the coordinating website with more tools and tips." *–Cyndi Maxey, MA, CSP, Speaker, coach, author, President, Maxey Creative Inc., Chicago, Illinois*

"Even the most successful leaders can be their own worst enemy when they buy into their self-limiting beliefs. When this happens leaders are not able to achieve optimal outcomes both personally and organizationally. Business leaders and professionals will benefit from Marcie's practical advice on how to develop and access the inner advocate that will support their overall work effectiveness and achievement of personal career goals. I have been on the platform with Marcie many times and she has always impressed me with her quality of thinking and compassion for the "good struggle" toward becoming a healthy and fully capable leader. She addresses a universal human struggle with both simplicity and grace. I urge you to read it." *–Doug McKinley, Psy.D., Xcellero Leadership.*

"So Long Inner Critic, Hello Inner Champion: 25 Tips to Master Your Mindset is filled with all those stories we repetitively tell ourselves – and yet, never want to hear. Marcie has offered us a simple to follow step-by-step path to guide us towards our own deep dark stories in order to flush out truths, accept what seems unacceptable, and ultimately, point us in a liberating direction through humor, ease and grounded action." *–Soleil Hepner, Self-care Expert & Educator*

"I love the concept of creating an inner champion to empower me to attain my highest goals. Marcie Stern's book, *So Long Inner Critic; Hello Inner Champion: 25 Tips to Master Your Mindset*, delivers substantial well-documented insights and ideas that work. Take Marcie's advice and you will soar to heights you didn't know you could reach." *–Dianne Morr, author of Choose Happy: 25 Happiness Habits to Transform Your Life*

"We all need to be reminded that there is no need to hinder our advancement within our career journey or with any of our relationships as a result of our inner critic but rather learn to manage it and flourish. Why be your worst critic when you can be your biggest supporter? Marcie guides you to your potential by providing simple tips on how to change the course of your mindset. Live the life you want to its fullest!" *–Toni Marnul, Creative Director, Reynolds Consumer Products*

"Marcie shares her personal triumph over her own inner critic which makes you realize you are not alone. She then provides practical tips to override the negative words and turn them into positives. She does not tell you what to do; she guides you to make your own choice which is the only way to truly become the strong, confident person you are. We started out this way and then we allowed our inner critic to take over. Marcie guides us back to our original self and helps us learn how to keep that inner critic quiet." *—Renee Hill, Warren Insurance Agent*

"As a wife, mom and career women, I often find life swiftly whizzing by. The tips in this book made me stop, think, and act with more intention. When I am present to my thoughts and actions and embrace both my inner critic and inner champion, I can find greater purpose and joy in life. Thanks for reminding me that God created me uniquely—and to relish in all the blessings He has provided." *– Lucy Zielinski, Vice President, Health Directions, Inc.*

"This is not your average self help book. It is a most useful compendium of 25+ excellent techniques we can all use to live a more gratifying and productive life." *– Ryan Schwartz, Chief Marketing Officer, US Assure, Zurich Insurance Services*

So Long Inner Critic
Hello Inner Champion

Tips to Master Your Mindset

Marcie Stern, MHA, RLC

Creator of the WAAMM™ Principle

Published by Marcie Stern & Associates

Cover design and interior book design by Debbie Mackall, Shine Visual Communications, Inc.

Author photo by Rich Master Photography

Stern, Marcie

www.marciestern.com

ISBN 978-0-9891271-0-3

Dedication

To my husband, Scott—you have always been my biggest fan and I'm enormously grateful for your unconditional love and support.

To my children, Matt and Nate—you are my greatest teachers and source of inspiration. You are mirrors reflecting my own self-talk and remind me daily the importance of modeling an ability to tap into the inner champion voice. I hope you always remember how special and magnificent you are and never allow your inner critic to lead your life.

To the late Rabbi Sherwin Wine whose influence on me was not fully realized until it was too late to thank him. He was one of the first to teach me the value of self-esteem and the importance of positive self-talk.

"Every person wants to feel worthwhile. Every person seeks to find his self-esteem. An individual who believes in himself and in his power to do good is the strongest of people. A person who despises himself and condemns his own talent is the weakest of human creatures.

Without self-respect there is no happiness. In the end, a person becomes what he thinks he is. The person who thinks himself worthy of life will live. The person who thinks himself worthy of death will destroy himself."
–*Meditation Services for Humanistic Judaism, Rabbi Sherwin T. Wine*

Table of Contents

Design The World Around You

Acknowledge Your Body

Stay Connected

Introduction

"Our deepest fear is not that we are inadequate. Our deepest fear is that we are powerful beyond measure. It is our light, not our darkness that most frightens us. We ask ourselves, 'Who am I to be brilliant, gorgeous, talented, fabulous?' Actually, who are you not to be?" *–Marianne Williamson*

I wrote this book for those who may find they are their own worst enemy;

> who have ever been limited by listening to their inner critic voice;
>
> who believe their inner critic voice is right;
>
> who have ever questioned that they–and their work–matter; and
>
> who are interested in creating a legacy they can be proud of by saying "so long" to their sabotaging voice and "hello" to their inner champion voice.

I am passionate about this topic because I have personally been limited by my inner critic voice. Since childhood, my inner critic told me that my opinions do not matter. When I allow that inner critic to spiral out of control its ultimate message is that "I don't matter." Despite a lifetime of academic success, numerous professional achievements, promotions at one of the country's most prestigious hospitals, and a strong professional reputation, I feared being discovered as not capable of handling my leadership positions or deserving of my successes.

You may recognize this phenomenon as the "Imposter Syndrome"–the persistent feeling that, despite [your] well-deserved success and accolades, [you] are somehow [a] fraud and will soon be exposed.[1] Essentially, it is the fear that others will find out you don't really know what you're talking about. For me, professionally, this meant that I remained silent in meetings and frequently deferred to the opinions of my senior leaders. Perhaps worst of all, this behavior invaded my personal life, and I realized my personal and professional lives were based on what others expected of me—not what I wanted for myself. I also recognized the following consequences if I continued to listen to my inner critic. I would:

- not contribute my best qualities;
- be disengaged from the people and work that matter most;
- resent those closest to me;
- bring my inner critic's negative energy into all the roles I played including wife, mother and professional; and
- present a role model for my children of living life according to others' expectations

This awareness was heightened when I trained as a professional coach. I felt drawn to using my newfound coaching skills professionally, and I was at a point in my life where I sought better work/life balance. I found ways to incorporate coaching in my work at the hospital, but I was hungry for more. The notion of switching careers was terrifying and it required that I face my inner critic head-on. It was time to change and let my voice be heard.

When I decided to leave my hospital administration career and launch my own business as a professional development coach, speaker and trainer, I immediately became less inhibited at work. I spoke up more in meetings and quickly learned that my leaders wanted that input from me all along. In making the decision to leave the hospital, I bade farewell to my inner critic in two ways:

1. I trusted my experience and opinions as relevant and worthy of attention; and

2. I trusted my decision to leave a promising career in order to create a personal and professional life that better suited my values, strengths, and passions.

Two benefits resulted from my ability to quiet my inner critic:

1. The hospital benefited from my insights and contributions

2. I created a more authentic life

Fast forward ten years. . . I changed careers, chose work that aligned with and leveraged my talents, learned to say "no," and created a balanced life that succeeds on my terms both personally and professionally. This success comes without compromising one area of my life for another and demonstrates how I've learned to say "so long" to my inner critic voice and "hello" to my inner champion voice. In addition, people now pay me to speak to them and coach them because they sense my authenticity and confidence. Don't get me wrong, my inner critic continues to tap my shoulder and get my attention. Fortunately, I am now experienced enough to access the toolbox of techniques presented in this book for noticing that voice, acknowledging it and sending it on its merry way.

As a professional development coach, speaker and trainer I have learned that most people are unaware of how much they listen to and buy into the message of their inner critic voice. It becomes a mindset—a fixed state of mind or mental attitude—that influences how they view their lives or particular situations and how they will respond to those situations. That mindset, more than anything else, sabotages their ability to achieve the goals that matter most.

Awareness of the inner critic voice is only the first step. You also need to build awareness around the stronger voice, what I call your "Inner Champion" voice—the voice that will serve as your advocate in the most challenging circumstances. Welcoming this voice allows the messages of your inner critic voice to fade. Awareness alone, however, is not enough to create sustainable change. You must make a conscious decision to consistently think and act in ways that strengthen your inner champion instead of reinforcing your inner critic. Choosing your inner champion means you are better positioned to make subsequent choices that align with your day-to-day priorities and larger life-long goals. The choice, as you will learn throughout this book, is yours.

In this book I offer some wisdom, simple exercises and "Mindset Musings" to help you bid farewell to your inner critic and welcome your inner champion voice. I'm convinced that tuning out your inner critic beliefs and turning up the volume of your inner champion voice will allow you to master your mindset, achieve goals beyond your imagination, and fully accept that you matter each and every day.

Throughout this book, you will see call-out messages titled, "Mindset Musings". These musings will reinforce the content in this book by providing complementary resources on the Master Your Mindset webpage, www.masteryourmindset.info. A complete list of Mindset Musings, along with the itemized resources, can be found on page 87.

Meet the Inner Critic

"One tiny mad idea can hijack our loving mindset."
–*Gabrielle Bernstein, Spirit Junkie*

Our inner critic is with us all day long. Perhaps your self esteem is lowest when you first wake up in the morning. For example, when you look at yourself in the mirror in the morning, does your internal voice say something like, "Bad hair day!" or does it sound more like, "You Rock!?" Imagine yourself driving to work and finding that you are low on gas. Do you automatically think, "You idiot, you should have filled up last night and now you're going to be late for work!" or do you simply accept that you may be late, made a mistake, and commit to never running below a quarter tank?

When you stop at your favorite coffee spot on the way to the office and the new barista messes up your drink order, does your inner critic say with a sulky tone of voice, "These things always happen to me" or might you think, "I'm a great customer to practice on since I'm so loyal and feel comfortable giving honest feedback?" And when at work if a colleague requests help on a project, do you think, "I better say 'yes' so my colleague likes and respects me" or do you confidently decline and suggest an alternative solution for your colleague?

Get the idea? Whenever I present the inner critic concept to my audience, I display a slide that lists the following possible definitions of "inner critic:"

- Self-sabotaging voice

- Running negative commentary

- Self-limiting beliefs

- Mind trash

- Condemning conscience

- The 'should' voice

- The judging voice

And when I ask, "Does anyone NOT know what I'm talking about?" I have yet to find an audience member who raises his or her hand.

We are all familiar with this judging, condemning voice. Some people are more adept at ignoring the voice's message and not allowing it to belittle them. But for others, it can dictate our mindset and inhibit our self confidence, self worth and degree of engagement in our personal and professional lives. Martin E.P. Seligman, PhD, founder of positive psychology and author of the book, *Learned Optimism: How to Change Your Mind and Your Life*, refers to the inner critic voice as "catastrophic thoughts."

Negative messages, life experiences, interpretations of life events, and social standards telling us how a successful life looks program us to constantly measure ourselves against these messages and standards. Over time, these messages strengthen and reinforce the inner critic voice. Additionally, we often go through life never questioning these beliefs but owning them as if they are part of our DNA.

Science tells us that we have about 60,000 thoughts each day, which equates to about one thought every waking second. Of those 60,000 thoughts, about 95% are habitual–that is, we unconsciously think the same thoughts over and over again. What makes this relevant to the topic of inner critic is that of those 95% habitual thoughts, 80% of them tend to be negative. This means we potentially have 45,000 negative thoughts each day! Dr. Daniel Amen—a world-renowned psychiatrist and brain imaging specialist calls them Automatic Negative Thoughts (ANTs).[2]

80% of our habitual thoughts are negative. This means we potentially have 45,000 negative thoughts each day.

What would be the impact on your life if you could reprogram and remove these negative or "catastrophic" thoughts from your thinking? Who would you be and what would be possible if these 45,000 daily thoughts supported, instead of sabotaged, your goals? What goals could you accomplish by mastering your mindset?

Chapter
2

Greet Your Inner Critic

"The bulk of the work in weakening your Saboteurs involves exposing them to the hot light of awareness by simply observing and labeling them when they show up." *–Shirzad Chamine, author of Positive Intelligence: Why Only 20% of Teams and Individuals Achieve Their True Potential and How You Can Achieve Yours*

Before you can say "so long" to your inner critic voice, you must become aware of what it is saying and how you are buying into the beliefs associated with its message. I love to say this is as easy as ABC–because Awareness Brings Change. It also brings Choice. As Maya Angelou says, "When you know better, you do better." But stick with me here because before you can actively quiet that incessant voice, you need to make some formal introductions.

Before you can say "so long" to your inner critic voice, you must become aware of what it is saying and how you are buying into the beliefs associated with its message.

Take the next couple of days or weeks to become familiar with your inner critic voice. This may come easier for some people based on individual levels of awareness, so take the time you need.

The following seven methods can be used to identify your most prominent and destructive inner critic voice:

Methods of Inner Critic Identification

1. Fill in the Blank

A personal development workshop I attended suggested that most of our inner critic voices can be summed up in the following two succinct phrases: [3]

"I'm too _____."

"I'm not _____ enough."

Some of these statements may sound familiar:

"I'm not good enough."

"I'm too old."

"I'm not smart enough."

"I'm too shy."

"I'm too impatient."

"I'm not successful enough."

"I'm too scared."

Take two to three minutes and fill in the blank to either one or both of these statements. Keep writing words–without judgment or edits–until your time is up or until you truly cannot produce any more words. Don't limit yourself to one aspect of your life. If it's easier, start with one minute focusing on your professional life and the next minute focusing on your personal life. When complete, review the phrases and note any key themes.

2. Listen for the "Shoulds"

Whenever you hear yourself think or say the word "should," that is a red flag that your inner critic is speaking. For me this sounds like the following:

I *should* go to the health club.

I *shouldn't* eat that dessert.

I *should* make at least five prospect calls each day to grow my business.

I *should* say "yes" to being a board member when asked by the organization's past president.

Do these "shoulds" sound familiar to you? For the next two weeks, write down every time you think or say the word "should" and see what inner critic or self-limiting belief is associated with that statement. For more insight, pair these findings with those found in Method #1 ("I'm too _____" or "I'm not _____ enough") to identify inner critic consistencies. For me, it would be paired with "I'm not doing enough." Sometimes, the "shoulds" in our lives are messages driven by society's standards that run counter to our core values. Therefore, also pairing this exercise with Method #6, "Name Your Values," will help if your "should" voice is linked to one of your core values.

3. Look for Symptoms

Do you consistently . . .

- Question the value you offer or the contribution you are making?

- Second guess yourself and your choices or go back on a decision you have already made?

- Let others' opinions hold you back from acting in the way you want?

- Procrastinate?

- Feel inhibited from taking action or speaking your mind?

- Ask for permission instead of forgiveness?

- Experience disengagement or apathy?

- Take feedback personally?

- Focus on past failures and regrets?

- Feel stuck personally or professionally?

- Ignore your successes and all that is going well in your life?

These are symptoms that an inner critic is influencing you. Consider behaviors that may hint at an inner critic thought. For example, I would second-guess my decision to resign from my hospital administration job when others around me had the opinion that it was too risky or an unwise career move.

4. Keep a "Trigger" Log

This method will help you identify triggers for your inner critic and resulting thoughts, beliefs and responses.

Keep a log for two weeks of what triggers a negative feeling or thought and document the resulting message. There may be a particular person or situation that renders you disempowered, defensive, afraid or manipulated. Admittedly, for me, there are a few people who trigger the "I'm not smart enough" inner critic feeling. Knowing this upfront, I'm better able to proactively reframe the situation such that I don't let the inner critic take over. For example, I may think to myself, "I'm doing the best I can with what I know."

5. Name Your Fears

Take two to three minutes and list all your fears. For example, what is your greatest fear in life or what stops you from taking action on your goals? Do you fear:

losing your job;

living alone;

speaking up;

keeping quiet;

not living up to your potential; or

your own magnificence?

See if there are any themes among your fears that may consistently be holding you back.

6. Name Your Values

It may sound strange to link "values" to the "inner critic", however, there exists an interesting relationship between the values and the principles we hold dear and our inner critic's messages. I describe this as the Value/Inner Critic Continuum.

Inner Critic   **Value**

Write down the name of your core values and find the name of the opposing "drama queen/king" to that value. For example, you may value excellence and high quality work. But when our drive is to excel and produce work that is always 100%, then the "perfectionist" inner critic may be at play. Sometimes I find this tendency when I'm working on my monthly electronic newsletter article. I may spend an inordinate amount of time and energy to perfect it for fear of what my readers may think if they find a typo. When fear or negative thoughts are motivating your actions, then your inner critic is running the show.

Ask yourself, "Where, on the continuum, do I tend to live? Who is making decisions for me?" If you give power to your inner critic, you are letting your condemning conscience influence your actions.

7. Sense it

Use your senses to get acquainted with your inner critic. This may come more naturally to some than to others. That's okay; try it anyway. Here are some exercises that may help you:

a. What does your inner critic sound like? What is its tone of voice (for example, is it whiny, obnoxious, pathetic, anxious)?

b. What do you see or notice visually? This may be metaphorical where you picture something or someone who embodies the essence of the inner critic.

c. If your inner critic had a taste or smell, describe it from those senses.

d. What feelings or emotions might you have that would suggest an inner critic voice is active?

Name it!

After you try on one or more of the above methods and are clear on what your inner critic sounds like, I highly recommend you give your critic its own name.   Let me introduce you to "Perfectionist Patty." She is one of my inner critic voices that says, "I'm not doing enough" and demands perfection in all that I do and in all the roles I play. I didn't realize how often and in what situations she gets my attention until I opened up and became aware of her message.

Before you can move forward with quieting the inner critic, you must face it head on and recognize that it is not completely separate from you. It has its own identity and, surprisingly, it's not the enemy. Accept that it may be there to raise a red flag to warn, protect, or even motivate you. As such, you don't want to entirely eliminate or ignore it. After all, the title of this book uses the phrase, "So Long" and not "Goodbye." Your inner critic is one of the ingredients that makes up who you are. You can't take the ingredient out of your favorite recipe and end up with the same result, but you can reduce the amount of that ingredient and create a new, more flavorful twist on the end product. And here's an important insight—if you do try to ignore your inner critic, it will most definitely not retreat quietly. In fact, ignoring it will incite it. As you will see in Chapter 5, naming your inner critic voice is like putting a bright light on an insect and watching it scurry away back into the darkness.

Understand Your Inner Critic Cycle

"The ancestor of every action is a thought."
–Ralph Waldo Emerson

"I can't do anything right. I am a failure. I am not worthy." This is my client Ellen's inner critic voice. Ellen is a rising star at a Fortune 500 company and recognizes that her inner critic voice is anchored in the fact that she became a mother when she was a teenager. Imagine the impact of her owning this mindset. Not only has it affected her professional life by preventing her from seeking higher level roles, it's also impacted her physical, emotional and mental well-being. It was only when she realized the long-term consequence of this way of thinking and her potential to pass it on to her two young children that she was motivated to shift.

Evaluating the impact of buying into your inner critic's message will serve as an important catalyst to shifting your focus. The Inner Critic Cycle diagram shows a cycle that will reinforce the inner critic unless you make a change.

It starts with an event; something in your life happens (and this could be as trivial as a driver cutting you off or as serious as doing work that is misaligned with your values). The situation generates an internal

The Inner Critic Cycle

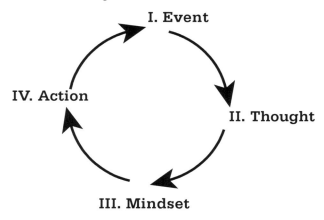

I. Event

IV. Action

II. Thought

III. Mindset

thought—words that you choose to either accept or reject as true. Based on this choice, you form a mindset—the sum total of your opinions and feelings attached to the thought and that becomes an outward expression of the thought. This mindset, or mood, influences your actions and behavior. The cycle exists when you are faced with similar situations that trigger similar ways of thinking, feeling and acting. For example, recall the last few times something happened that triggered you to feel that life was unfair and you always get the short end of the stick. How did you respond? Chances are that such triggers–regardless of the specifics of the situation–generated a similar behavior. This is how our habitual way of thinking (remember the ANTs–"Automatic Negative Thoughts") perpetuates the cycle and the result is more of the same–more of what you probably don't want in your life. To break the inner critic cycle, choose a different thought that develops into a more positive mindset.

"You attract to your life whatever you give your attention, energy, and focus to, whether wanted or unwanted."

As Michael J. Losier, author of *The Law of Attraction. The Science of Attracting More of What You Want and Less of What You Don't* describes, "You attract to your life whatever you give your attention, energy, and focus to, whether wanted or unwanted." While we don't always have control over the event, we most definitely have control over our response to the event. Creating thoughts that support rather than sabotage us, will ultimately translate into more productive outcomes.

Breaking the Inner Critic
Example: Ellen's Inner Critic Cycle

Event: Teen-age mom

Thought: I did something I wasn't supposed to do.

Mindset: I'm a failure, worthless and undeserving.

Action: Stay stuck at work; model low self-esteem to children.

Breaking the Inner Critic Cycle for Ellen may look like the following:

Event: Teen-age mom

Thought: Cool! I have more energy as a young mom to do more things with my daughter.

Mindset: Positive, creative, spirited, focused.

Action: Request that boss discuss career development opportunities; become fully engaged with daughter.

Here's a personal example

Event: My birthday five years ago. Two sons with a day off school eating cookies in my car and dropping crumbs all over the backseat.

Thought: The boys are being messy and inconsiderate.

Mindset: Annoyed and feeling dumped on because I will need to clean the car when we get home when I have so many other things I need to be doing.

Action: Critiquing; suggesting alternative ways to eat the cookie so crumbs don't go all over the backseat

Breaking the Inner Critic Cycle for me actually looked like the following:

Event: My birthday five years ago. Two sons with a day off school eating cookies they are getting along in my car and crumbs going all over the backseat

Thought: They are thoroughly enjoying their cookies, they are getting along, and I'm so lucky to be sharing this day with them.

Mindset: Gratitude and joy for having these two amazing boys as my sons

Action: Telling the boys, "I love you and thank you for sharing my birthday with me."

The impact of our self-sabotaging voice is that it limits our abilities and potential, making us afraid, resentful, angry, powerless and feeling like a victim. Based on the science of ANTs, we will continue to see our life's situations from the same negative perspective because that is what we have trained ourselves to do. Eric Allenbaugh, Ph.D. and author of *Wake-up Calls*, says, "When you empower self-limiting beliefs, you limit your potential. When you argue for your limitations, all you get is your limits – and you stay stuck."

"When you empower self-limiting beliefs, you limit your potential. When you argue for your limitations, all you get is your limits – and you stay stuck."

To stop this negative cycle, evaluate the costs and benefits of your habitual negative thoughts (i.e., consequences). Oddly enough, we do get some benefit from holding dearly to these thoughts (for example, receiving sympathy from others when we feel we've been wronged or feeling safe by not stepping out and taking risks). However, these benefits tend to be short-lived and we don't consider the longer-term consequences.

Using the inner critic names you created from Chapter 2, "Greet Your Inner Critic," write down all the benefits and costs of owning your inner critic beliefs and the related actions and behaviors that support these beliefs. This will give you some objectivity and clarity to make a more conscious choice to either reinforce or break the Inner Critic Cycle.

Mindset Musing #2: *Inner Critic Cost/Benefit Worksheet*

Chapter
4

Debunk Your Inner Critic Myth

"We are disturbed not by what happens to us, but by our thoughts about what happens." –*Epictetus, Greek Philosopher*

My teenage son, Matt, believes he is not athletic. This thought first entered his consciousness when he was hit by a ball in Little League practice at the impressionable age of six. During that practice, another player swung his bat and accidentally hit Matt's arm. Since that day, Matt believes that he and sports do not mix well, which quickly translated to, "I'm not good at sports." This is the story Matt continued to tell himself and whenever he faced any athletic encounter, he interpreted the events in the same way.

In middle school eight years later, Matt had to complete one of those "All About Me" assignments which included three statements describing himself. It was not surprising to see "I'm not athletic" listed as one of Matt's three statements. Several months later he decided to join the track and field team at school. Matt is tall, fast and strong. Track and field seemed like a great opportunity for him to use those attributes and challenge himself physically. On the first day of practice, he wiped out on the track and skinned up several areas of his body. He vehemently proclaimed, "See, I told you! I'm not good at sports!" This conclusion was the only possible way for him to view the situation. It is the story he had been telling himself repeatedly for eight years (notice the Inner Critic Cycle).

This chapter can be challenging but also extremely liberating. It's where you get to debunk the myth of the inner critic by understanding its source, then challenging whether or not it is true. Because of the Inner Critic Cycle described in Chapter 3, "Understand Your Inner Critic Cycle", we tend to hold on to our beliefs as truths. Our inner critic voice is convincing because it owns and repeats the story, thought and belief over and over again. How we continue to interpret our experiences validates and reinforces the inner critic.

Like Matt, we prove ourselves and our theories right, because we continue to interpret our life's events in a way that we have previously defined. It never occurs to us to stop and question, "Is this thought or belief really true?" And though it's not a necessary step to quieting our inner critic, it is helpful to understand the origin of that belief and to debunk the myth of all that that story symbolizes.

Often, a situation at a very early age (typically by age five or six) leads us to own a belief about ourselves, about others, or about the world in general. I invite you to dial back the clock and search your earliest memory that created the self-limiting beliefs that hold you back.

Follow this exercise to debunk the myth of your inner critic.

1. Review your list of inner critics

Go back to those you identified in Chapter 2, "Greet Your Inner Critic"

2. Choose the most significant

Start with the one that is the most significant block to your success. You can go back and follow the same steps with the other inner critic names.

3. Identify the situation

Recall a recent time when this belief showed up. Describe the circumstance, other people involved, your beliefs, your actions and your response to the situation. Repeat this process going back just six months, then two years, five years, ten years, and so on, until you reach the earliest memory of this belief occurring (again, this usually surfaces around age five or six).

4. Ask, "Is the belief true?"

Was this belief true back then or was it just one way in which a five-year-old's mind interpreted the situation? Could there be other possible interpretations?

5. Ask yourself, "Who's running the show?"

Now consider that your five-year-old self (or whatever age you were when you first recall thinking this belief) is dictating what you believe to be true about yourself today and impacting your ability to achieve important goals. Isn't this perspective interesting as we step back and see the genesis of our working minds? You may even find it to be comical or ridiculous that your five-year-old self is running the show.

Note: this exercise may require some additional time and coaching. It is not to be taken lightly as it may reveal a situation that is highly emotional and sensitive. If that is the case, then I encourage you to work with a professional coach or therapist for support in unveiling a significant past experience that holds you back from accomplishing your goals and creating a legacy of which you can feel proud.

"I am not what has happened to me.
I am what I choose to become." –*Carl Jung*

Other Influential Factors
Creating Inner Critic Beliefs

Self-limiting beliefs don't always come as a result of our own experiences but are often told and reinforced by others. Some examples include authority figures such as our parents, clergy, and teachers, or more generally from society or the media. We may inherit others' beliefs just by being around them, listening to them and being influenced by them in some way. For example, women may have been taught that it's impolite to toot their own horn; corporate women may be led to believe that there's a glass ceiling preventing them from serving as leaders in their companies; or rightsized, out-of-work professionals may believe that it will take at least 12-24 months to find new employment that matches their talents and interests.

To help debunk the myth of any self-limiting belief, ask yourself these five questions:

1. "Is it true?"

2. "Where did I learn this?"

3. "What is the impact of buying into this belief?"

4. "Do I choose to adopt this belief as my own?"

5. "Who defies this belief?" (Is there someone I know, or someone in society that is doing the very thing that I believe to be impossible?)

You may also find that your inner critic beliefs are a direct result of others giving you messages that could have been communicated in jest but are interpreted as damaging. I shudder when I hear parents label their children in such ways that may have long-term repercussions. For example, parents tell their child, "You're trouble with a capital T!" or "You're a wild child!" or "You are accident prone." Even positive sounding messages such as "You are smart" can negatively impact a young impressionable mind. The interpretation may be, "If I want to make my parents proud I must outperform or get all A's." You can see how this type of thinking can be fodder for one's inner critic voice. When you find yourself in a situation when your interpretation directly aligns with your five-year-old's story or is based on what others have told you, get in the habit of separating

When you find yourself in a situation when your interpretation directly aligns with your five-year-old's story or is based on what others have told you, get in the habit of separating the situation and your interpretation.

the situation and your interpretation. Use the Inner Critic Cycle diagram to whittle the event or the incident down to the bare facts and recognize that everything else is simply your interpretation. This will give you more power to choose a perspective that will support you.

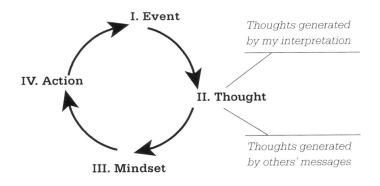

"Perception is a choice and not a fact."
–Marianne Williamson, A Course in Miracles

Mindset Musing #3: *Rewrite History Exercise*

Chapter
5

25 Tips to Master Your Mindset

"Taming your gremlin has absolutely nothing to do with out-arguing him or with being right… It has to do with simply noticing; choosing and playing with options; and being in process."
–*Richard Carson, Taming Your Gremlin: A Guide to Enjoying Yourself.*

Despite knowing that your inner critic is a creation of past experiences, stories, and interpretations stemming from you and others, it is challenging to simply dismiss it as a myth–like some stranger on the street you pass by–and move on unaffected. The following tips are a collection of techniques gained not only from personal experience, but from other experts in the fields of positive psychology, neuroscience, and performance coaching.

The tips have been categorized to help you select those that may be of interest but I also encourage you to select a variety.

- The "Build Your Foundation" tips are important groundwork and highly recommended.

- The "Train Your Brain" tips require some degree of action either by writing, speaking or acting.

- The "Design the World Around You" tips are techniques to surround yourself with a supportive environment–both physically and with people.

- The "Acknowledge Your Body" tips are action tips but also require you to use your body in some way.

- The "Stay Connected" tips are more about your state of mind—the "being" instead of the "doing".

I suggest starting with "Build Your Foundation" tips #1 and #2. Then try the others on one at a time—give it a few attempts before deciding if the technique works for you or not. Saying "so long" to the inner critic will likely require utilizing more than one technique and using it over time (at least 30-60 days) before the effects take hold. I have also noted suggested pairings of strategies that often work well together.

1

Hello Inner Critic…
Name and Notice
Your Inner Critic Voice

"Only when we're brave enough to explore the darkness will we discover the infinite power of our light." – *Brené Brown, Ph.D., LMSW*

Though it sounds counter-intuitive, I want you to welcome in your inner critic voice. It's important to acknowledge and not suppress, ignore, or fight it. The old saying, "That which you resist persists" couldn't be truer when it comes to fighting your inner critic because guaranteed, the inner critic will win.

We go through great efforts in naming our children and then our children are equally selective in naming their favorite stuffed animals. As suggested at the end of Chapter 2, "Greet Your Inner Critic," naming your inner critic voice(s) is an important first strategy. It's helpful to step back and think of your inner critic as separate from you and naming it is an effective strategy to create that distinction. For ideas on possible inner critic names, I encourage you to read *Taming Your Gremlin* by Richard Carson or *Positive Intelligence* by Shirzad Chamine.

Creating a separate identity for your inner critic will help you notice and then disassociate from it–from its thoughts, beliefs, tone of voice, atti-

Creating a separate identity for your inner critic will help you notice and then disassociate from it—from its thoughts, beliefs, tone of voice, attitude, expectations, and so on.

tude, expectations, and so on. You can increase your objectivity by acknowledging it as separate from you. This will make your decision to choose a different direction easier. You may even find yourself being empathetic towards this new identity—knowing that it was born from an impressionable child's interpretation of his or her world. A great way to build on this technique is to create a biography for the inner critic after it has been named. Tell his or her story and include a picture of it. You can hand-draw your own picture or simply search on key words in Google Images until you find one that embodies the essence of your inner critic.

Let's look at my personal example of one of my inner critic names, "Perfectionist Patty." She sure has high expectations and loves it when everything is perfect. She is good for keeping me connected with my values for quality at home and at work. But she can be exhausting and downright damaging if I let her take over all my thoughts and actions. Imagine my reaction when she berates me for not booking a new speaking engagement and for not serving healthy, delicious, well-balanced meals for my family each day.

2

Hello Inner Champion…
Name Your Inner Champion Voice

"It takes courage to grow up and become who you really are."
                            –E.E. Cummings

Kevin Cashman, author of *Leadership from the Inside Out*, defines the inner voice as "the one in your gut, the impulse that speaks to you through feelings, inspirations, intuitions and possibilities." The notion that your intuitive voice is the same as your inner champion voice may be an effortless connection to make. You may automatically link that voice to a divine or spiritual source and, if that's the case, then name that voice as your inner champion voice. But for others, this may still feel elusive.

It is not uncommon that identifying and naming your inner champion voice is more challenging than naming the inner critic—because the latter voice is the one to which we most gravitate. Since you will likely have more than one inner critic voice, you can identify an opposing, inner champion voice name to each one. If you read *50 Shades of Grey* by E.L. James, you know that the protagonist, Anastasia, named her inner champion voice, the "Inner Goddess."

Here are two exercises to help you name your inner champion voice:

1. Return to the Values/Inner Critic Continuum and refer to the "value" opposite your inner champion voice. For example, if I notice "Perfectionist Patty" getting my attention, I can shift to "Doing My Best Diva" which reflects my value around consistently striving to produce quality results while acknowledging that perfection is unattainable.

2. Identify three key qualities that reflect your ideal self—the qualities you most want to demonstrate in any situation. Then incorporate those qualities into one or more inner champion voice names.

Once you have named your inner champion voice, invest the same degree of energy and thoughtfulness you would normally give to your inner critic voice. The idea is to put your attention into thoughts and beliefs that will support you, not sabotage you. Whenever you find yourself listening to your inner critic voice, consciously choose to tune into the inner champion voice instead. For added impact, have a picture or other physical reminders available that will serve as a prompt for focusing your energy on your inner champion voice.

Example

~~**Inner Critic: "Perfectionist Patty"**~~   **Value: Quality Results**

Inner Champion: "Doing My Best Diva"

Physical Reminders:

1. Say out loud, "I'm doing the best I can."

2. Read quotation on a post-it note: "Progress, not perfection"

3. Review weekly documented progress on goals

3

Hello Core Strength…
Stay Grounded in Values and Vision

"Things that matter most must never be at the mercy of things that matter least." –Johann Wolfgang von Goethe

The degree to which you are grounded in your core values, a personal vision, and meaningful goals is the degree to which you are able to let go of the inner critic beliefs and prevent them from taking residence in your psyche. Recall the relationship between the inner critic and your core values. It's important to know where you are on that continuum and to purposely shift toward the value end and away from the inner critic end. A good litmus test question to ask is, "Where on the continuum is this feeling, thought, or choice?" If it's closer to the inner critic end, then use the following techniques to shift and stay grounded in the value side.

The degree to which you are grounded in your core values, a personal vision, and meaningful goals is the degree to which you are able to let go of the inner critic beliefs and prevent them from taking residence in your psyche.

1. Identify your core values. Questions to consider include:

    a. What is most important to me?

    b. What must I have in my life to feel fulfilled?

    c. What do I stand for?

2. Have a clear vision or set of goals for the important areas of your life (particularly those that are most impacted by your inner critic).

3. Reinforce your values and goals by using visual representations including:

   - Vision board (a visual representation or collage of your dreams and goals);

   - Framed personal mission statement (refer to Tip #4, "Develop and Incorporate a Personal Mission Statement");

   - Screen saver;

   - Photographs;

   - Favorite quotations/mottos visually displayed (refer to Tip #11, "Use a Mantra"); and

   - Other physical items that symbolize your values/goals (e.g., family heirloom, souvenir from a vacation/special time in your life).

Mindset Musing #4: *Values Inventory Exercise*

Hello Purpose…
Develop and Incorporate a Personal Mission Statement

To forget one's purpose is the commonest form of stupidity."
–Friedrich Nietzsche

"When she looks at you, you know you've been seen. When she listens, you know you've been heard." This is how I recall Oprah describing Michelle Obama when she interviewed her soon after Michelle became First Lady (for the first time). These are words that I long to have people use to describe me, so the essence of this phrase is evident in my own personal mission statement.

My personal mission statement is: "To be fully engaged with those who cross my path and to inspire people to see, own and leverage their magnificence. I do this by acknowledging others for their gifts and challenging them to fully utilize those gifts in creating a successful life on their terms."

If you are grounded in your core values and possess an ideal vision of your life you have a foundation for creating a mission statement. This is your personal brand–a positive and concise statement of how you want to impact others and how you want to be known. Every company I ever worked for has a mission statement, but rarely do people have one of

Knowing how you intend to live your life and honor your values gives you a significant advantage in your life—not only will it provide direction, but it will keep you on track even when you face obstacles along the way.

their own. A mission statement can serve as your moral compass guiding you even during the most turbulent of times when your inner critic voice is screaming at the top of its lungs. Knowing how you intend to live your life and honor your values gives you a significant advantage in your life—not only will it provide direction, but it will keep you on track even when you face obstacles along the way. Those that are clear about their purpose and life mission tend to be happier and more successful on their own terms.

There are several approaches for creating a mission statement. First, answer one or more of the following questions to help identify key words or phrases for your mission statement:

- What legacy do I want to leave behind?

- How do I want others to describe me?

- Who or what matters most to me?

- What are my core values?

- How would I define success in my life?

- What makes my life really worth living?

- What must happen in my life to feel fulfilled?

- What do I long to master?

Using the above insights, fill in the blanks of this mission statement template:

"I impact others by _____ (insert the type of legacy you want to create). I do this by being someone who is/does _____ and _____ (insert strengths or qualities you have and express or would like to use in fulfilling on your legacy)."[4]

Or more simply, complete the following phrase: "My personal mission is to _____."

A third technique is to write your own obituary or eulogy. Recently, I learned that a woman I went to high school with died from a long bout with breast cancer. I was told she wrote her own obituary and it took my breath away. I have no doubt that she lived her life in complete alignment with the written words because of her forethought in creating them. This exercise may sound a bit morbid but it can help you get very clear on the above questions. If that feels too challenging, then imagine it's your 90th birthday and there's a big celebration with family, friends and colleagues from your working days. Write a speech that you would want a member from each of these groups to recite at the party.

Once your mission statement is developed, keep it visible. Read it, say it out loud and imagine each and every day living in complete alignment with the statement. If you can do this habitually, you will notice quickly that the inner critic's voice will be drowned out by a more powerful force.

5

So Long Eeyore; Hello Tigger...
Replace the Negatives with Positives

"A man is but the product of his thoughts.
What he thinks, he becomes." *—Mohandas Gandhi*

My client Suzanne recently proclaimed, "I'm realizing the power of my habitual thoughts!" She noticed since engaging in a coaching partnership that she took greater responsibility for her thoughts. During our coaching, she found herself working a second job to supplement her income. This situation would have naturally led her to think, "I have to do this" and that thought would have resulted in her feeling like a victim—disempowered and resentful. Instead, she created and practiced this new thought about the job, "This is a great opportunity to learn something new," which gave her renewed energy and optimism.

I first encountered the "Erase and Replace" technique from the book, *What to Say When You Talk to Yourself* by Shad Helmstetter. The concept is simple and reinforces the earlier message that we can't ignore the inner critic nor can we say, "I just won't think those thoughts anymore." If we use that approach, then we create an empty space. Because we have created a habit of listening to the beliefs of our inner critic's Automatic Negative Thoughts, those beliefs will eventually re-establish their residence in our psyche, and we are back to incorporating those old stories into every cell of our body. This technique may remind you of the books, *Eat This, Not That* by David Zinczenko. The "Master your Mindset" version could be titled, "Think This, Not That."

The science behind the technique of "Erase and Replace" is called neuroplasticity. Neurpolasticity is the "capacity of neurons and neural networks in the brain to change their connections and behavior in response to new information, sensory stimulation, development, damage, or dysfunction. Neuroplasticity occurs when neurons in the brain sprout and form synapses. As the brain processes sensory information, frequently used synapses are strengthened while unused synapses weaken." [5]

If we feed our brains with new words and new emotions relative to those words, then over time, we will believe them and act in a way that aligns with those beliefs.

Here are four steps to incorporate the "Erase and Replace" strategy:

1. Log and keep track of what your inner critic says (and the situations and/or people that trigger it). You can refer to the Trigger Log from Chapter 2, "Greet Your Inner Critic."

2. Write a key inner critic phrase or belief on one side of an index card.

3. On the backside of that index card, write something else you can say to yourself to counter that belief.

4. Practice saying and thinking the counter words whenever you hear the inner critic voice. It may feel awkward at first and require you to "fake it 'til you make it."

The best way to move quickly out of the "fake it" phase is to engage as many senses as you can when you speak or think the counter words. Know what it looks like, feels like and sounds like to fully adopt this new way of thinking and the benefits of doing so. Another way to say this is to "visualize" the words being active in your life.

To advance this visualization process, I recommend doing the following three "S" steps:

1. Scribe: Write out the new words and thoughts. Refer to step #3 in the previous exercise.

2. Speak: Voice out loud the new words and thoughts so you can hear yourself claiming the words and owning them.

3. Share the new words and thoughts with someone you can trust. This will further reinforce them and build accountability in the process.

With practice and frequent repetition, these more empowering messages will soon be accepted and the need for the index cards to serve as a reminder will diminish.

Example: When I don't complete my work to-do list, my inner critic tells me: "You're not doing enough," "You should be doing more," or "You're not working hard enough." Replacing these thoughts with "I'm doing the best I can" or "I'm closer to my goal today than I was three months ago" helps shift my mindset. And if speaking these words is not enough, I will sit quietly for a few minutes, breathe deeply and visualize how the progress I've made has impacted my clients.

6

Hello Applause...
Keep a Success Journal

"Too many people overvalue what they are not and undervalue what they are." *—Malcolm Forbes*

"I'm not there yet. I'm a work in progress." I hear this frequently from clients when checking on their progress toward their goals. So often we focus on what isn't working in our life rather than what is and that kind of behavior fuels the fire of the inner critic mindset. When I focus on what I didn't complete or accomplish in a day, it reinforces the message that "I'm not doing enough." The reason, according to Rick Hanson, Ph.D., neuropsychologist and author of *Buddha's Brain: The Practical Neuroscience of Happiness, Love, and Wisdom*, is that "the mind is like Velcro for negative experiences, and Teflon for positive ones. Our brain has a 'negativity bias' that continually looks for, reacts to, and stores negative experiences."

> **"The mind is like Velcro for negative experiences, and Teflon for positive ones. Our brain has a 'negativity bias' that continually looks for, reacts to, and stores negative experiences."**

Have you ever received an evaluation or performance review where all you hear is what you can be doing better instead of what you have done well? Consider the typical one-hour performance review. The first five minutes may be focused on your accomplishments from the previous year while the following 55 minutes is spent reviewing the gaps in your performance and discussing strategies for improvement. These formal evaluations only exacerbate the inner critic voice. Instead, make sure you take time to focus on successes. And in a performance review situation, that may mean supplying evidence of your accomplishments.

Here are three ways to shift your focus on what is going well:

1. Each day, write down three things that you did well (for example, engaging in a positive conversation with a loved one or colleague, completing a project-related task, or making a decision that aligns with your goals).

2. Focus on and visualize the impact of those accomplishments (for example, how those things align with your inner champion voice and mission statement).

3. Maintain a Word document or manila folder for "Accomplishments" and keep track of your successes, big and small. This is useful for performance reviews and will boost your confidence when you feel you are not achieving or contributing enough.

I maintain a folder in Outlook called "Gratitude" and populate it with emails from clients and audience members who provide positive feedback. In those moments when I find myself focusing on what isn't going well, I will click open that folder and be quickly reminded of all the lives I've touched in positive ways.

Refer to Tip #16, "Express Gratitude" as another strategy for focusing on what's working well.

Mindset Musing #5: *"Ta-Da List"*

7

So Long Exaggeration...
Make an Appointment with Your Inner Critic

"The more we refuse to buy into our inner critics - and our external ones too - the easier it will get to have confidence in our choices, and to feel comfortable with who we are. . ." –*Arianna Huffington*

When I facilitate the "Energy for Life" program for Allstate Insurance employees,[6] I make a distinction between the Winnie the Pooh characters Eeyore and Tigger to illustrate two opposing mindsets. Eeyore, the constant pessimist, looks down on himself and on life while Tigger is consistently joyful and optimistic. Winnie the Pooh stories wouldn't be what they are without Eeyore as a main character—he is part of the package just as our inner critic voice is part of us. But have you ever considered what Tigger would long to say to Eeyore to knock some optimistic sense into his droopy head?

If your inner critic loudly and repeatedly represents the consistent negative mindset of Eeyore, then stop resisting the inner critic. Welcome it in and let its voice be heard. But, here's the important part—set a time limit for the inner critic to be heard.

I recommend carving out about 10 minutes for this exercise.

1. Use a blank piece of paper. Draw a vertical line down the middle. On the top left side write "Inner Critic" and on the top right side write "Inner Champion "

2. Set a timer for three minutes.

3. Begin by writing down everything on the left side that your inner critic is telling you about the situation. You can write phrases, words, full sentences or use bullet points but just keep writing until the three minutes are up. Continue writing for up to two more minutes if your inner critic has more it wants to say.

4. Read what you wrote out loud.

5. Set the timer again for another three minutes and on the right side of the page, contrast everything you wrote on the left side. Again, use more time if necessary.

6. Read everything you wrote on the right side out loud.

This exercise brings awareness to the distorted, and often ridiculously exaggerated, thinking of your inner critic and immediately shifts your attention to the alternately supportive and healthy thoughts and beliefs you wrote down. Writing down your inner critic thoughts gives you the opportunity to create distance and objectivity. Remember, as stated in Chapter 2,

Writing down your inner critic thoughts gives you the opportunity to create distance and objectivity.

"Greet Your Inner Critic," don't ignore the inner critic because it will only scream louder until you have no other choice but to listen. Recognizing it and giving it its due time shines the light on it to the point where you can acknowledge and then deal with it. By the way, this is one of my favorite strategies!

8

Hello Showstopper…
Communicate Consciously

"The interpreter in you tells the story in a way nobody else can—with your voice, your body, and your selection of words." -- *Cyndi Maxey and Kevin E. O'Connor, Present Like a Pro*

Here are four ways that more conscious communication can help you quiet your inner critic:

1. Use positive language

Think before you speak. We often don't pay attention to the words we use and the manner in which we speak them. It's important to choose your words intentionally and carefully. Anytime you think or speak out loud, notice the following:

"I should."

"I can't."

"It's not worth it."

"It's not possible."

"I have to."

"I'm not [fill in the blank] enough."

"I'm too [fill in the blank]."

41

Practice rephrasing with more positive language including: "I want," "I choose," "I am," or "I am becoming."

Practice rephrasing with more positive language including: "I want," "I choose," "I am," or "I am becoming." This may feel awkward at first, but with repeated practice, you will find yourself using more positive, empowering lan-guage naturally—whether it's what you say to yourself quietly or out-loud to others.

2. Speak authentically

Have you ever tried to communicate in a way that doesn't really sound like you? You may be adopting someone else's style—someone that you admire or are inspired by. This may work on the surface, but ultimately you feel phony and your inner critic may take over. Furthermore, others may not connect with you as well and/or may not see you as a credible or influential communicator. Find ways to communicate that feel natural to you but will also connect with others based on their own styles. This combination will boost your confidence as an effective communicator and result in others' connecting better with your ideas and messages.

3. Communicate effectively, especially in difficult situations

The inner critic can really be loud when we are faced with a difficult conversation or conflict. Consider how much more effective you can be if you engaged in a difficult conversation or conflict with a strong mindset and inner champion voice. This positions you for a highly successful interaction between you and the others involved in that exchange. One technique you may have heard is called the "When, Feel, Want" method. It helps make the situation more about you than the other person so there is less opportunity for defensiveness.

Dave, a client, told me how he used this technique at work with his colleague, Pam, who interrupted him to impart her own wisdom. Here's how Dave handled the communication: "Pam, when you interject your opinions and ideas before I have finished speaking, it makes me feel as though you aren't listening to me and that what I'm saying is not relevant to the conversation. Next time we discuss an issue, hear me out completely before responding—or at least check in with me first to see if I have finished expressing my thought."

There are several excellent books on effective communication. I highly recommend *Crucial Conversations: Tools for Talking When Stakes are High* by Kerry Patterson (lead author) so that your inner critic doesn't speak for you in these challenging situations.

4. Express yourself visually as a strong communicator

The words you speak are important, but even more important is the tone of voice and nonverbal ways in which you communicate. Research conducted by Albert Mehrabian, Ph.D. Professor Emeritus of Psychology at UCLA, indicates that when communication involves feelings, attitudes, likes and dislikes, then both verbal and nonverbal messages contain relative importance. His formula, Total Liking = 7% Verbal Liking + 38% Vocal Liking + 55% Facial Liking[7] means that the actual words we speak have minimal influence when communicating feelings and attitudes. However, the way our words sound coupled with our nonverbal cues and body language contributes greatly to our ability to communicate feelings and attitudes effectively.

In consideration of Mehrabian's research findings, it is worth taking note of how your body language influences how others perceive you and your message. If your mindset is focused on your inner critic, then your body language will likely follow suit (i.e., poor posture, no eye contact, crossed arms or an aggressive, in-your-face type body position). Couple that with the following three scenarios and you could be compromising as much as 93% of your effectiveness:

1. Feeling inhibited and speaking in a quieter tone of voice;

2. Feeling nervous and having a fast-talking style; or

3. Feeling defensive and speaking with a loud, sharp tongue.

I shared this research with my client, Sam, who had been rightsized out of a job. Sam had an excellent resume, credentials, and network to support him on his job search. He felt that he could sell himself much more easily in person than on the phone. He was not being effective converting warm lead phone calls to informational or job interviews because his predominate thought as he dialed was, "Why would they want to talk to me? I'm wasting their time." And his body language matched his inner critic's thought. Sam decided to tap into his inner champion voice as well as change both his vocal tone and body language. He put a picture of his family by the phone, sat up straight in his chair, smiled as he dialed and spoke with sincere authority. I checked in with Sam two weeks later and was not surprised to learn he had a job offer in hand.

Mindset Musing #6: *Communication Style Assessment Tool*

9

Hello Curiosity...
Challenge **Your Inner Critic**

"A thought is harmless unless we believe it. It's not our thoughts, but our attachment to our thoughts, that causes suffering." *–Byron Katie*

When you hear your inner critic getting your attention, reflect fully on what it is saying. Get curious and ask if the belief is true. Is there evidence to suggest it is true? And if you have a hard time convincing yourself that the opposite could be true, then find evidence to support that. For example, if I start buying into the belief that it's not possible to effectively balance my work and personal life without compromis-

Challenging the inner critic belief places you in a position to deflect it and move forward, which in turn helps tone down the negative message and turn up the volume on what is possible.

---

ing one or the other then I will find plenty of examples of people who I admire that are doing just that. And even if I find myself thinking "Yes, but . . ." at least it gives me an opportunity to discredit my inner critic belief and choose another, more positive belief. Challenging the inner critic belief places you in a position to deflect it and move forward, which in turn helps tone down the negative message and turn up the volume on what is possible.

An excellent resource for challenging your inner critic belief is Byron Katie International's, "The Work." It consists of asking yourself the following four questions about your beliefs:

1. Is it true?

2. Can you absolutely know that it's true?

3. How do you react when you believe that thought?

4. Who would you be without the thought?

The next step is called "The Turnarounds" where you turn your statements around and have an opportunity to experience the opposite of what you believe to be true. For each turnaround find at least three specific examples where the turnaround is true for you. This is not about blaming yourself or feeling guilty. It's about discovering alternatives that can bring you peace.

Used with permission by Byron Katie

Mindset Musing #7: *"The Work" and "Judge-Your-Neighbor Worksheet"*

10

So Long Speed Racer…
Push "Pause"

"The right word may be effective, but no word was ever as effective as a rightly timed pause." –*Mark Twain*

Wouldn't it be great if we could push "pause" on our thoughts as easily as we push "pause" on a YouTube video when we want to take a break? Doing this as negative thoughts and beliefs are attempting a takeover gives you a moment to separate from what's triggering your inner critic and choose another path.

Once you have recognized the inner critic voice, say or think "Next" or "So what?" This creates a natural separation between old, negative beliefs and thoughts while creating space and providing you with an opportunity to regain control and shift to a different, empowering mindset. It also allows you to use more positive language as Tip #8, "Communicate Consciously" suggests (for example, "I choose _____." or I am becoming _____. ")

In my business, I teach the WAAMM™ principle. WAAMM™ stands for "What Actions and Attitudes Matter Most." It's a principle that helps busy professionals focus on what matters most by aligning empowering attitudes with focused actions and holding themselves personally accountable for their results. One client told me she started to overreact to an email she received and the message that she inferred from the sender's content. She literally thought to herself the word, "WAAMM™" and realized that this was not a situation on which she wanted to invest any energy. As a result, she let go of the inner critic thoughts, refocused on those things that mattered most and saved herself a great deal of stress and anxiety in the process. Choose a word or a phrase that will allow you to push "pause", reflect, and course correct.

11

Hello Inspiration…
Use a Mantra

"Just keep swimming. Just keep swimming. Just keep swimming, swimming, swimming." *–Dory, Finding Nemo*

School teachers may find their jobs to be both rewarding and challenging. One of my clients is a middle school teacher who focuses predominately on the demanding children in her classroom and the increased administrative expectations. This focus created such a negative mindset that she began second-guessing her career choice and seeking alternative career paths. To shift to a more empowering mindset, she decided to create a special jar filled with statements reflecting the positive experiences of teaching (for example, funny things students have said or done, feedback from a parent). Then when a challenging situation triggered her desire to be doing something different with her life, she read one of the slips of paper, took a few deep breaths and quickly reconnected with her passion for teaching and inspiring children in creative ways.

Reading or speaking a favorite mantra out loud ("a word or phrase that is repeated often or that expresses someone's basic beliefs"[8]) or saying a quotation when you notice yourself dipping into inner critic thoughts gives you an immediate opportunity to shift your mindset. Keep such words or phrases visible so they are readily accessible in all your familiar places–for example, post-it notes near your work space or on your bathroom mirror and in rooms of your house that you most frequent. Like my client, you could also decorate a container that serves as a repository for empowering and nurturing thoughts and beliefs. Write or print your quotations or mantras on slips of paper and select one from the container just before you encounter a potential trigger or after your inner critic voice has been triggered. Give this tip an extra boost by visualizing yourself acting in accordance with the words and phrases–especially in relation to the immediate trigger. For example, when I take time to work out or attend a yoga class, my inner critic will condemn me for taking time away from other priorities, such as family or work. The mantra that I say in response to that inner critic is, "Me-time is soulful, not selfish."

Set a morning intention for how you want your day to unfold; include your mantra or quotation to ground you and keep your mindset focused on what you want and how you choose to act.

Set a morning intention for how you want your day to unfold; include your mantra or quotation to ground you and keep your mindset focused on what you want and how you choose to act.

Combine this tip with Tips #2, #3, and #4 for added benefit.

Mindset Musing #8: *"Positive Mindset Quotations*

12

Hello Ghandi...
Speak or Act as a Mentor
or Inspiring Person

"For every problem, there is a solution." *–Scott E. Stern*

When you hear your inner critic talking loudly, imagine sharing its message with someone who embodies kindness, compassion, dignity and respect. This could be a famous person–like Mother Teresa or Ghandi–or someone in your life like a coach, teacher or professional mentor. What would this mentor or inspirational person say to you? It may help to write down his/her words. Now repeat those words to yourself out loud several times and visualize how the situation looks by owning that new, empowered message.

My husband, Scott, is a great role model for resiliency. When life throws him curve balls, he has incredible perseverance and is able to stay committed to the end goal. One way he is able to keep life's challenges in perspective is to say, "For every problem, there's a solution." Scott is a constant inspiration to me for many reasons, but especially when I'm faced with obstacles. I can hear that phrase ringing loudly in my ear and it immediately brings a sense of calm and shifts my mindset.

Another frequently used phrase that works for me is, "Put your big girl panties on!" I sometimes imagine Oprah saying that to me and it instantaneously gets me out of any inner critic funk and energetically moving toward my goals.

13

Hello Discomfort…
Act in Reverse

"If you hear a voice within you saying, 'you are not a painter,'
then by all means paint and that voice will be silenced."
–Vincent Van Gogh

My friend, Andrew, is an Ironman athlete with a natural zest for life. In November 2011, he experienced a heart attack. Fortunately, his body was so well conditioned that the heart attack did not result in long-term health consequences. Eleven months later, Andrew ran his first post-heart attack marathon. At mile marker 13, he was feeling the physical stress of the run in his knees. He started to question his body's ability to fully bounce back from the heart attack and support him in completing the race. Andrew immediately noticed being hijacked by his inner critic voice and turned it around by taking on his Ironman mindset and attitude. He told himself he could do it, had done it and despite the physical pain that he may experience, had what it took to push through it and complete the marathon. Those opposing thoughts guided him the remaining 13.2 miles and allowed him to complete his fourth marathon.

During my training with The Coaches Training Institute, my classmates and I were asked to demonstrate one quality that our clients could benefit from, but was personally uncomfortable for us to express. It had to represent a manner of behaving that was opposite to our natural behavior. Before we had the opportunity to engage in a ten minute coaching demo to try this quality on, we had to give the trait a name, write it on a "Hi, My Name is _____" nametag and wear the nametag for the remainder of the day. My nametag read, "Bad Ass" because I am polite and tactful, and believed this was something I could not do or be. But this trait is necessary for coaches in pushing their clients further and holding them accountable to achieve their goals. Practicing being "Bad Ass" felt truly uncomfortable because it was in complete opposition to my natural way of interacting with people. But the more I incorporated "Bad Ass" qualities into my coaching (in a very compassionate way, I must add!) the more comfortable and confident I became in holding my clients accountable and contributing to their success.

While it may feel risky and uncomfortable, acting in a way that completely contradicts your inner critic belief can help you grow your inner champion voice muscle.

While it may feel risky and uncomfortable, acting in a way that completely contradicts your inner critic belief can help you grow your inner champion voice muscle. Jim Loehr, Ph.D. and author of *The Corporate Athlete Advantage: The Science of Deepening Engagement* suggests that the extent we stretch beyond our comfort zone, is the degree to which we will grow. It requires pushing beyond your current capacity in much the same way you would build your bicep muscle at the gym. The muscle will only grow if you continuously challenge it by steadily increasing the weight you lift.

If your inner critic says you are too shy, then act in an extroverted way—do or say just one thing that feels bold. This is similar to the "act as if" principle where you exhibit a behavior of the person you want to be and, as your actions become habits over time, you achieve the desired way of being. Taking opportunities to act in ways opposite to what your inner critic says will quickly negate that belief, give you more confidence and strengthen the muscle of your inner champion voice. This tip pairs nicely with Tip #2, Name Your Inner Champion Voice.

14

Hello Popeye…
Focus on and Leverage Your Strengths

> "People have several times more potential for growth when they
> invest energy in developing their strengths instead of correcting
> their deficiencies." —*Tom Rath, Author, Strengths Finder 2.0*

After I receive a speaker evaluation, I spend more time agonizing over the one negative comment than all the positive comments. When I focus on areas of weakness, it reinforces the message that "I'm not good enough." If you experience something similar, it's because your inner critic gets a rush out of putting the spotlight on your weaknesses.

As mentioned in Tip #6, "Keep a Success Journal", the reason for our natural ability to focus on weaknesses first is based on the notion by Rick Hanson, Ph.D., that "the mind is like Velcro for negative experiences, and Teflon for positive ones." Following that tip's suggestion to write down three things each day that went well also applies here. Writing down and focusing on how you used your strengths each day will leave you feeling more in control and empowered.

To help reveal your signature strengths, complete the following three statements and questions:

1. Name three to five skills/strengths you credit yourself with having. How have they positively impacted you personally and/or professionally?

2. Name three to five skills/strengths others would say you demonstrate. What positive impact would others say they have had?

3. What accomplishments have others praised you for? What skills/strengths were demonstrated in those accomplishments?

Mindset Musing #9: *Strengths Inventory*

15

So Long People-Pleaser…
Say "No"… Gracefully

"…it's only by saying 'no' that you can concentrate on the things that are really important." *–Steve Jobs*

Do you know people who work 60+ hour weeks, are raising children, are actively involved in their communities through volunteering and maintain an active social life? Do you know people who have a difficult time saying "no" when asked to take on more work, assist a colleague in a project, volunteer and then find themselves feeling over-committed, overwhelmed, and burned out? Are you currently sitting in the seat of someone just like that?

"No"—a simple two letter word—is one of the more difficult words to express especially if you are a self-proclaimed people-pleaser or perfectionist. Here are 10 strategies for learning to say "no" directly and gracefully.

1. **Use a litmus test question**. Ask yourself, "Will saying 'yes' to this request move me closer to or further away from my values and immediate goals?" or "Would I be saying 'yes' more out of fear about how others will perceive me if I say 'no' or because this action fully aligns with my values and priorities?"

2. **Have a personal policy.** Companies are great about having and promoting policies to define what they can and cannot do in various situations. Consider how a personal policy could help you create boundaries so that you are not over-extended. For example, I have a policy that unless I'm traveling for work, I will not be away from my family for more than one night a week. That makes me more selective when it comes to engaging in networking, social outings or volunteer activities.

3. **Pause before answering.** Sometimes, just giving yourself a few seconds to take a deep breath before answering with a resounding "Yes!" is enough to allow you to collect your thoughts and respond more effectively.

4. **Delay your response.** This is different from the "pause" technique and means that you can acknowledge the request (see "Use flattery" below) and ask for some time to consider it before answering. This will buy you some time to be thoughtful in determining if a "yes" is the best answer.

5. **Use flattery.** Most of us feel flattered that others think of us when requesting us to do something they feel we'd be good at. Acknowledge this by saying, "Thank you; I'm flattered that you think highly enough of me to make that request." And then use another technique – like the personal policy – to gracefully decline the request.

6. **Offer an alternative solution.** You can soften the blow of saying "no" and still feel that you're making a contribution by offering another solution or person to fulfill the request (and make sure you have that person's permission first!)

7. **Postpone.** If the request is something that aligns with your values and goals but the timing is not right, offer a future time when you may be in a position to say "yes."

8. **Delegate.** This can be a tricky one, especially if you are a perfectionist (or dare I say, control-freak?) Clearly, others will not do the job in the

same way you would but consider the benefits. For example, delegating to employees increases their level of confidence and allows them to be more engaged and empowered while freeing you up to focus on your priorities.

9. **Conduct a cost/benefit analysis.** Write down the costs–both short and long-term—of saying "yes" when you would rather say "no" as well as the benefits.

10. **Swap out.** If you choose to say "yes" to a request, recognize that you may need to swap that out by saying "no" to something else.

Start building your "saying no" muscle with something simple this week. The more you are able to say the word "no" the easier it gets and the more liberated you will feel.

16

Hello Appreciation...
Express Gratitude

Feeling gratitude and not expressing it is like wrapping a present and not giving it." –*William Arthur Ward*

When you are focused in the present moment and can demonstrate gratitude for all that is going well in your life and all that you have, there is little room for any inner critic thoughts.

Expressing gratitude is a great way to drown out the inner critic voice. When you are focused in the present moment and can demonstrate gratitude for all that is going well in your life and all that you have, there is little room for any inner critic thoughts. Writing in a gratitude journal is a great technique for transferring what you may feel gratitude for into a more structured manner. The exercise of writing it down forces you to fully acknowledge those things for which you are grateful. It gives what you write down more power so you can easily focus on those things rather than the "what's missing" or "what's wrong" list. Creating a habit of gratitude trains you to perceive situations more positively. And the more you interpret life this way, the more you will exponentially attract positive events into your life. It's a gratitude cycle worth starting.

Try it out. Take one minute to write down everyone and everything you are currently grateful for. It doesn't have to be the big stuff – find gratitude in a really good parking spot on a rainy day or a perfectly made latte or a text from someone you love that says, "I love you." You may find it difficult to stop at one minute.

Whenever you notice an inner critic thought entering your mind-set, whip out a piece of paper, open up a Word document, or open up the notes APP on your Smartphone and express gratitude!

17

So Long Psychic Vampires...
Banish Negative People
From Your Environment

"Keep away from people who try to belittle your ambitions. Small people always do that, but the really great make you feel that you, too, can become great." *–Mark Twain*

There are three groups of people who may be reinforcing your inner critic:

1. **Psychic vampires.** These people literally suck the energy from you. I took the commuter train every day when working in downtown Chicago and would invariably sit near a group of people who complained incessantly about their jobs—about their bosses, their peers, the work they did, their office space—you name it and it was fodder for critique. The desire to physically move away from that negative energy was overwhelming.

   I'm sure you can relate as you consider being at work or in a social situation when you "felt" the negative energy from a group of people even without hearing exactly what they were saying. Unfortunately, psychic vampires don't exist just outside your inner circle of family, friends and colleagues; they very well may be people you know (and live with!) You may surround yourself with psychic vampires unknow-ingly and can easily be influenced by their negative views on life. Over time, these people will only reinforce your own negative thoughts. Therefore, it is important to set boundaries around how much time you spend with these people or, if possible, eliminate them entirely from your inner circle.

2. **Negative Nellies.** These people in your inner circle may also be a form of a psychic vampire because if they tend to be a glass-is-half-empty person, then they will view you, your life and your choices in the same way. People who are unhappy or insecure in their own lives will easily find fault in and critique others. Negative Nellies—or as my husband, Scott, likes to call them, "Deputy Downers"—may even be outspoken in highlighting your own insecurities and inner critic and use the exact words your inner critic voice does such as: "What were you thinking?"or "That would be impossible!" or "You can't do that!"

3. **Media Mania**. The media in general (digital, print, video) can easily reinforce our inner critic messages because it often portrays an ideal vision of what we and our lives "should" look like. It's impossible to live up to many of the societal messages (think cover photos of wom-en's and men's magazines . . . need I say more?) On top of which, the media tends to focus on negative messages based on the notion that sensationalism and fear sells. For example, we hear negative mes-sages like, "It's impossible to find a job in this economy" or "Work/life balance is a myth." My suggestion is to not expose yourself to these messages. However, when the message occurs, be careful how you interpret it and how you apply it to your own life.

Recognize you may not fully eliminate these people and messages from your life but limiting your exposure to them and setting boundaries will help reduce their influence on your mindset and messages. As Tip #5, "Replace the Negatives with Positives" suggests, you will need to re-place those people and sources of media with others who can (and do) affirm you and honor your inner champion voice and authentic self. Fur-thermore, you will want at least one to two people to be your go-to ac-

You will want at least one to two people to be your go-to accountability partners who will help you get control of your inner critic.

———————————————

countability partners who will help you get control of your inner critic. This would be someone you can call or text right away when your inner critic voice is grabbing your attention and who can acknowledge you for where you are, but will also help move you out of your inner critic thinking. This person is your "ANT (Automatic Negative Thought) Exterminator."

Children make great accountability partners and ANT Exterminators. First, they love to catch us when we don't keep our commitments or role model positive behaviors, so they will happily let us know when we are off track. Second, they are a wonderful reminder of the positive aspects of our life and can quickly put our sabotaging inner critic thoughts into perspective.

My pre-teen son, Nate, is a great ANT Exterminator for me. He constantly tells me that I'm beautiful, loving, and the best mother in the world. Once, while we were hugging good night, he said, "I feel sorry for you mom because you don't know what it feels like to be hugged by you." It's nearly impossible to allow self-limiting beliefs to invade my mindset while being on the receiving end of Nate's heartfelt compliments. If you don't have a child in your home or one of your own, my suggestion is to borrow one! Grandchildren, nieces, nephews, and neighbors' kids will work too!

Mindset Musing #10: *Supportive Environment Template*

———————————————————————————————————

18

So Long Clutter…
Create a Supportive Physical Environment

"Your sacred space is where you can find yourself over and over again." *–Joseph Campbell*

Have you ever noticed how your physical environment often supports your inner critic? Scan the room you are in right now (assuming you're not in a public space). Whether you are at home or in your office, does the space contribute to you feeling small, unworthy or in ways that reinforce your inner critic? Notice too how the space you surround yourself with may reflect what's happening in your life. Is it cluttered and disorganized; is it tidy and "perfect"; is it dusty; or does it need a makeover? The space you inhabit can be a good signal of how you are feeling and acting in your life.

If you have created an environment that reflects your inner champion voice, are you actually tuning out the positive messages? For example, my office has plenty of inspiring quotes, photos of my family and visible acknowledgements from those whose lives I've touched. But rarely do I take in and appreciate these positive visual reminders. Just spending one minute to read a "thank you" note, gaze into the eyes of my children in a photo or reflect on fond memories of a favorite vacation can immediately change my mindset to one of gratitude and empowerment. Design a sacred space—whether that's a focal point of a room or an entire room—have some physical space where you can reframe any negative thoughts and feel grounded.

Mindset Musing #11: *Ideas to Create a Supportive Physical Environment*

19

Hello Harmony...
Listen to Inspiring Music

"Music can change the world because it can
change people." –*Bono, U2*

If you are moved or inspired by music, this is a great tip for you. I am one whose self-limiting mindset can change rapidly if I listen to an upbeat, up-lifting, no-one-can-stop-me type of song. One of my favorites is "Defying Gravity" from the musical Wicked. Consider these lyrics: "It's time to trust my instincts. Close my eyes and leap... I think I'll try defying gravity and you can't pull me down!" And, if a situation leaves me feeling stressed or frustrated, calming music such as pianist, George Winston, works great for slowing me down and gaining new perspective.

What's your theme song? What songs would be included on your "sound-track of life?" Have a playlist of songs that will immediately have you saying, "so long" to your inner critic and "hello" to your inner champion. To get even greater benefit from this tip, sing along with the song and add a few dance moves as suggested in Tip #21, "Move Your Body."

20

So Long Stress...
Breathe

"Breathe and breathe again.
In every breath we are remade." *–Unknown*

Stop what you are doing right now and notice your breath. How would you describe your breathing—is it short, long, tight, or relaxed? If you engage in inner critic thoughts, then your breathing will likely be more shallow or constricted. This is often the case when we are feeling stressed about a specific situation or more generally about the demands that we, and others, place on our lives. Athletes are skilled at using their breath to prepare for and recover from demands being placed on their bodies. Have you ever noticed that they take a few deep breaths just before and after engaging in something that requires them to be focused and exceptional? Think about tennis players before they serve the ball or a basketball player before throwing a free-throw or a gymnast before mounting an apparatus. Those breaths help them shift out of potential self-defeating thoughts ("I better win this point if I have any chance

If you engage in inner critic thoughts, then your breathing will likely be more shallow or constricted.

at winning this match") to more positive, winning thoughts ("I can do this!"). You can apply a similar method when you feel that the demands on your life are eliciting negative beliefs and the inner critic voice.

> When you notice negative thoughts and/or behavior, stop and take some deep breaths. Put your hand over your belly, close your eyes and take five to ten deep breaths allowing your belly to rise on the inhale. Try it now. Inhale on the count of four and exhale on the count of six. This is diaphragmatic breathing. You may also put your other hand over your heart during this exercise and speak a personal mantra (refer to Tip #11, "Use a Mantra"), cite your mission statement or repeat a calming/grounding word (like "om").

You could plan such breathing activities to ward off an imminent inner critic attack. Think about the people or situations you identified in Chapter 2, "Greet Your Inner Critic" (the "triggers") and incorporate this diaphragmatic breathing exercise before you encounter that person or situation.

Mindset Musing #12: *Breathing and Meditation Techniques*

21

So Long Slump...
Move Your Body

"Let's dance, let's shout. Shake your body down to the ground."
–Michael Jackson

Whether you are currently sitting or standing in this moment, purposely put your body into a withdrawn and slumped position. Keep your head down, round your shoulders, do not make eye contact with anyone and frown. Stay in this position for a few moments and notice how it feels. While not so exaggerated, this is potentially how your body may be positioned if your inner critic leaves you feeling fearful, cautious or timid. Consider what your body is doing when each of your inner critic voices has your attention. Being aware of how your body is positioned when you are fully engaged in your inner critic thinking will give you the opportunity to reposition your body – and mindset.

Now imagine yourself fully embracing a new, empowering mindset. Move your body in a way that is associated with those thoughts. Or, recall a time when you felt confident, strong and courageous. Replicate right now how your body was positioned during that time. You may notice that you sit or stand taller; have a lifted head, brighter eyes and smile; your chest is out; and you emit a sense of pride and confidence.

Even if you can't fully adopt this mindset, position your body in this manner anyway and you may notice that this subtle shift in your body will automatically force you to have more positive or empowering thoughts. And if you can't decide what your body would look or feel like in that empowered position, you could always engage in a yoga Mountain Pose. It's a great pose that generates a sense of core strength and feeling grounded.

Moving your body may also mean getting some kind of physical exercise, whether it's a short walk, a jaunt up and down a stairway or a full work-out. You may have heard that our brains release endorphins during physical exercise which means we not only reap physical rewards, but we gain emotional benefits as well. Endorphins released through regular exercise can result in stress reduction, improved self-esteem, and positive emotions.

Try dancing as a way of moving your body and shifting out of an inner critic attack. Dancing is a great method for expressing yourself authentically. So turn up the volume to your favorite dance music and dance as if no one is watching. Whether this makes you feel empowered, free, or even silly, guaranteed it will shift you out of your inner critic beliefs. (Warning . . . don't try this option if you know you'll be overly critical of your dance moves . . . or lack thereof!)

22

Hello Body…
Tune in to Your Body

"The body says what words cannot."
—Martha Graham, Dancer and Choreographer

Mounting evidence suggests the existence of a "mind/body" connection. The benefits of understanding and leveraging this powerful connection can contribute to a well-balanced, happy and healthy life. Most of us are not tuned in to our bodies and accept minor aches and pains or a cold or flu as part of life. Actually, our bodies constantly give us messages when we are feeling both good and bad.

I am a firm believer that our bodies speak to us when we have been listening to our inner critic voice. For example, when I feel overwhelmed and imperfect in my abilities to effectively juggle family, work and community commitments, I notice that my upper back and shoulders get tense as if I were "carrying the weight of the world on my shoulders." Do you know anyone who suffers from low back pain? That can often be attributed to not feeling supported – or feeling like they are the only one who can get things done the way they want them done.

Listening to your body can provide helpful insights about your thoughts and beliefs. Below are three steps that will help you 1) build awareness of your mind/body connection, and 2) produce both healthy thoughts and a healthy body.

i. Become aware of what your body feels like in both positive and negative states of mind. When you are feeling exuberant, confident and grateful, how does your body feel? Compare that to when you feel overwhelmed, worried or angry, or when you allow your inner critic to control your decisions and actions.

ii. When you notice an ache or an illness, inquire more thoughtfully about what your body may be telling you. If your body shows physical signs of ill health, ask "What belief do I have about my life right now that may be contributing to this situation?" There's never a good time to be sick or injured but consider a time when you said to yourself, "I can't afford to be sick now; I have too much going on" and then became sick. It could be your body's way of telling you that you need to ease up and take care of yourself. I often hear about such illnesses happening after an important event such as a wedding, a vacation, or a significant work presentation or project. It's as if we ask too much of our bodies and then they are forced to put us in recovery mode. In this way, our bodies may be sending us clues that we've been honoring our inner critic.

iii. The goal is to maintain a healthy body through proper nutrition, exercise, and sleep. When you take care of your body, your mind will feel healthier and mentally and emotionally rested. You'll be less inclined to allow inner critic thoughts to invade your mind or body. It creates good karma because when you learn to honor your inner champion voice instead of your inner critic, you will undoubtedly take good care of your physical body.

A great resource for learning more about the mind/body connection and learning how negative thoughts may be impacting you physically is the book, *You Can Heal Your Body* by Louise Hay.

23

Hello Now…
Be Present

> "If you can concentrate always on the present, you'll be a happy man…because life is the moment we're living right now." *—Paulo Coelho, The Alchemist*

Jill, a mother of three and a human resources leader for a small business beamed at the beginning of our coaching session with this observation, "I am learning to be more present and in the moment and am finding that I'm more patient with others and myself as a result." You have probably heard a lot about "being present" and "living in the moment." But what does it really mean and how do you achieve a state of presence? Many of us have regrets about the past and will spend an inordinate amount of negative energy there, while others invest their inner critic energy worrying about and planning for the future. Rarely, however, do any of us fully accept and appreciate where we are today or even in this one and only precious moment. I'm reminded of the saying, "The past is not a place of residence, but a place of reference."

One technique for learning how to be "in the moment" is to practice diaphragmatic breathing.

Build on Tip #20, "Breathe" by focusing only on your breath. Sit in a comfortable position –no crossed legs or arms—and close your eyes. Place one hand over your belly as you inhale slowly, notice your belly rising and as you exhale slowly, notice your belly retreating back toward you r spine. Breathe in slowly, allowing your belly to expand. Try doing this on the count of four and then exhale slowly on the count of six allowing your belly to fall back. Keep breathing in and out in this manner and maintain focus only on your breath. Let all other thoughts float away and stay connected to your breath. Start by practicing this deep breathing exercise for one minute and then add more time as you get more experienced focusing only on your breath.

This practice will increase your ability to slow down and be more focused on the present moment.

24

Hello Choice...
Choose Consciously

"Our lives are a sum total of the
choices we have made." *—Wayne Dyer*

If all else fails, always remember that you are in control of your thoughts and have the ability to choose your mindset.

If all else fails, always remember that you are in control of your thoughts and have the ability to choose your mindset. You may want to reflect on your values/inner critic continuum. Where are your thoughts landing? If they are on the inner critic side of the continuum, ask yourself what it feels like to be there. Engage in a cost/benefit analysis exercise, and given the results of your analysis, make a conscious choice about your thoughts. Use Tips #5, #7, #11 and #12 to help fuel your mind with alternative, more empowering thoughts. In particular, Tip #5, "Replace the Negatives with Positives" suggests using the index card technique. When you write down two opposing thoughts (one on each side of the index card), you will visually see the choice as you read both sides of the card. The thoughts are not competing for your attention – it's ultimately in your hands (literally and figuratively) which thoughts you choose to occupy your mind. As Marianne Williamson said in *A Course of Miracles*, "You cannot be faithful to two masters who ask conflicting things of you."

If you are having a hard time conjuring up a different way to perceive a situation, reach out to your ANT Exterminator (refer to Tip #17, Banish Negative People from Your Environment) and brainstorm about other perspectives you may try on to define the situation. Remembering that you have a choice on your thoughts is liberating. It will give you an enormous sense of control and that's a great place to be when you want to say "so long" to your inner critic.

25

Hello Humor…
Lighten Up and Get Some Perspective!

"This I conceive to be the chemical function of humor: to change the character of our thought." *–Lin Yutang*

Step back and notice how ridiculous your fears and worries are when they are inflated and untrue. Many of the previous twenty-four tips allow you to separate yourself from your inner critic thinking and see these thoughts more objectively. This can be especially true after completing Tip #7, "Schedule an Appointment with Your Inner Critic". It is then that you can accept them for what they are and get some comic relief. Mark Sanborn, in his book, *Up, Down, or Sideways: How to succeed when times are good, bad, or in between*, suggests that finding humor is part of creating an "Optimist's Orientation" and being successful in life. He says, " . . . laugh at life because in our humility we realize we don't control everything." And if you can't see the humor in your situation or inner critic thinking, be sure to infuse some humor into your life–view a funny YouTube video, watch an old sitcom or engage in some good old fashioned joke-telling. There's nothing like a few minutes of robust laughter to lift your spirits and feel the lighter side of life.

Mindset Musing #13: *Bonus Tip: The INNER Process*

Chapter
6

Make a Personal Commitment

"Success isn't based on what we know, believe, or intend;
it's a result of what we consistently do."
*—Mark Sanborn, New York Times Best Selling Author
and Leadership Development Expert*

When I read books and find a wealth of information that leaves me with many highlighted phrases and/or dog-eared pages, it feels a bit overwhelming as I consider where and how to incorporate the lessons I've learned. It is not that we are starved for information, it's that we need a plan for applying that information in meaningful ways.

Since it takes approximately 30-60 days to break old and/or create new habits, I am providing a suggested eight week plan for incorporating insights you may have gained from this book. Shifting your attention and saying "hello" to your inner champion voice and "so long" to your inner critic will take consistent discipline and practice until new habits have been formed.

It is not that we are starved for information, it's that we need a plan for applying that information in meaningful ways.

1. **Week 1: Name the inner critic**

    a. Start with naming your inner critic(s)

    b. Recognize the impact those negative messages are currently having on your life.

    c. Evaluate the long-term consequences of continuing to buy into your inner critic message (Hint: this should give you the motivation to start taking action!)

    The tips provided in this book will not be applicable until you take this first, crucial step.

2. **Week 2: Create a plan for translating tips into action**

    a. Select three tips that you will try out over the next 30 days.

    b. For each tip, write down how and when you will apply the tip–for example, identify certain people or situations that you know you will encounter.

    c. Prepare materials you will need to support the application of each tip (for example, index cards, worksheets, pictures).

    d. Share your commitment with an accountability partner.

3. **Weeks 3-8: Track your progress**

    You've heard that what gets measured gets done, so it's important to track your commitment to applying the three tips including what worked, what didn't and why.

    a. Document progress in any way that suits your personality (for example, pen and paper or on the computer).

    b. Share your progress and insights on what worked/what didn't work and why with your accountability partner once a week. I recommend setting a regular day and time to talk with your accountability partner.

c. Modify as necessary. Brainstorm with your accountability partner on ways to eliminate barriers and/or leverage successes.

d. Celebrate your successes, no matter how small. As Tip #16, "Keep a Success Journal" suggests, it is easy for us to focus on what's not working instead of what is working. I encourage you to celebrate all your successes, no matter how small, as you notice how you have successfully bid farewell to your inner critic and welcomed your inner champion voice. Invite your accountability partner to do the same by acknowledging your progress.

"Nothing of significance occurs until you commit."
–*Mary Manin Boggs*

Mindset Musing #14: *Sample Tracking Tool*

---

4. Optional: Share your results with me.

I'd love to hear your progress as you Master Your Mindset! Email me at mstern@marciestern.com.

Also, throughout this eight week period, access the resources noted in the Mindset Musings. Refer to page 87 for a complete list to gain further insights and support.

Final Thoughts

This book may be a major wake-up call to the sound of your inner critic voice. Or, it is a gentle reminder that there are certain people or situations that reinforce your inner critic's message and make it challenging to acknowledge your inner champion voice. I hope you see the value in first building awareness of the inner critic voice before you can welcome the inner champion voice. For any change to occur, that awareness must be translated into action. Use the tips provided as if they were tools in your toolbox. Some tips may be more appropriate for certain situations. Test them out, and see which ones work best for you. Use them consistently until you are in the habit of accessing your inner champion voice.

My ultimate wish is that you choose to listen to the voice that will advocate for your magnificence. It is then that you will:

- master your mindset;

- demonstrate authenticity;

- provide the world all your amazing gifts; and

- have a successful life on your terms.

Best wishes on your journey to Master Your Mindset!

"Be careful of your thoughts,
for your thoughts become your words.

Be careful of your words,
for your words become your actions.

Be careful of your actions,
for your actions become your habits.

Be careful of your habits,
for your habits become your character.

Be careful of your character,
for your character becomes your destiny."

–Author Unknown

Recap of 25 Tips

Build Your Foundation

Tip #1: Name and Notice Your Inner Critic Voice

Tip #2: Name Your Inner Champion Voice

Tip #3: Stay Grounded in Values and Vision

Tip #4: Develop and Incorporate a Personal Mission Statement

Train Your Brain

Tip #5: Replace the Negatives with Positives

Tip #6: Keep a Success Journal

Tip #7: Schedule an Appointment with Your Inner Critic

Tip #8: Communicate Consciously

Tip #9: Challenge Your Inner Critic

Tip #10: Push "Pause"

Tip #11: Use a Mantra

Tip #12: Speak or Act as a Mentor or Inspiring Person

Tip #13: Act in Reverse

Tip #14: Focus on and Leverage Your Strengths

Tip #15: Say "No". . . Gracefully

Tip #16: Express Gratitude

Design The World Around You

Tip #17: Banish Negative People from Your Environment

Tip #18: Create a Supportive Physical Environment

Tip #19: Listen to Inspiring Music

Acknowledge Your Body

Tip #20: Breath

Tip #21: Move Your Body

Tip #22: Tune in to Your Body

Stay Connected

Tip #23: Be Present

Tip #24: Choose Consciously

Tip #25: Lighten Up and Get Some Perspective!

Mindset Musings

Throughout this book I referenced "Mindset Musings"—opportunities for you to dive deeper into a topic and access complementary resources. The Mindset Musings and resources are available at **www.masteryourmindset.info.** I do offer a bonus tip—not printed in this book, so be sure to take a look at Mindset Musing #13!

Chapter 2: Greet Your Inner Critic

Mindset Musing #1: Sample Inner Critic Trigger Log (p. 8)

Chapter 3: Understand Your Inner Critic Cycle

Mindset Musing #2: Inner Critic Cost/Benefit Worksheet (p. 15)

Chapter 4: Debunk Your Inner Critic Myth

Mindset Musing #3: Rewrite History Exercise (p. 22)

Chapter 5: 25 Tips to Master Your Mindset

Mindset Musing #4: Values Inventory (p. 30)

Mindset Musing #5: "Ta-Da List" (p. 38)

Mindset Musing #6: Communication Style Assessment Tool (p. 44)

Mindset Musing #7: The Work and Judge-Your-Neighbor Worksheet (p. 46) www.thework.com

Mindset Musing #8: Positive Mindset Quotations (p. 50)

Mindset Musing #9: Strengths Inventory (p. 56)

Mindset Musing #10: Supportive Environment Template (p. 64)

Mindset Musing #11: Ideas to Create a Supportive Physical Environment (p. 66)

Mindset Musing #12: Breathing and Meditation Techniques (p. 69) www.soleilhepner.com

Mindset Musing #13: Bonus Tip: The INNER Process

Chapter 6: Make a Personal Commitment

Mindset Musing #14: Sample Tracking Tool (p. 81)

Endnotes

[1] Kanazawa, Satoshi, "Why Do So Many Women Experience the "Imposter Syndrome"? Why rejection and disapproval are harder for women. December 13, 2009, The Scientific Fundamentalist and re-printed in Psychology Today (http://www.psychologytoday.com/blog/the-scientific-fundamentalist/200912/why-do-so-many-women-experience-the-imposter-syndrome)

[2] Amen, Daniel, Change Your Brain, Change Your Life: The Breakthrough Program for Conquering Anxiety, Depression, Obsessiveness, Anger, and Impulsiveness

[3] Landmark Education

[4] Mission Statement Template compliments of Ingrid Wallace Presents (www.ingridwallacepresents.com)

[5] Merriam-Webster.com http://www.merriam-webster.com/dictionary/neuroplasticity

[6] Human Performance Institute's The Corporate Athlete® Course

[7] Mehrabian, A. (1981). Silent messages: Implicit communication of emotions and attitudes. Belmont, CA: Wadsworth, and Mehrabian, A. "Silent Messages" –A Wealth of Information About Nonverbal Communication. http://www.kaaj.com/psych/smorder.html

[8] Merriam-Webster Learner's Dictionary http://www.learnersdictionary.com/search/mantra

Recommended Resources

- *Daring Greatly* by Brené Brown
- *Now, Discover Your Strengths* by Marcus Buckingham
- *Taming Your Gremlin* by Richard Carson
- *Positive Intelligence^{SM}* by Shirzad Chamine
- *Go Positive! Lead to Engage* by Sam Glenn, Doug McKinley, Psy.D. and Scott Carbonara
- *Buddha's Brain: The Practical Neuroscience of Happiness, Love, and Wisdom* by Rick Hanson, Ph.D.
- *You Can Heal Your Body* by Louise Hay
- *What to Say When You Talk to Yourself* by Shad Helmstetter
- *Feel the Fear and Do it Anyway* by Susan Jeffers, Ph.D.
- *Brag: The Art of Tooting Your Own Horn Without Blowing It* by Peggy Klaus
- *The Power of Story* by Jim Loehr
- *Speak Up! A Woman's Guide to Presenting Like a Pro* by Cyndi Maxey and Kevin E. O'Connor
- *Choose Happy: 25 Happiness Habits to Transform Your Life* by Dianne Morr
- *Crucial Conversations* by Kerry Patterson et al
- *Up, Down, or Sideways* by Mark Sanborn
- *Learned Optimism: How to Change Your Mind and Your Life* by Martin Seligman
- *The Untethered Soul* by Michael Singer

Visit **www.masteryourmindset.info** to access a variety of resources that will support your personal Master Your Mindset journey.

Gratitude

This book would not be possible without the generous time and energy invested by many friends and colleagues. I'm so grateful to have their support and guidance in helping me bring my first book to fruition.

I need to thank my family first. They have been incredibly supportive, especially since this book has often taken me away from evening time with them. It is heartwarming to know that they truly are my biggest supporters.

My sister, Soleil Hepner, has probably received more frantic phone calls and emails throughout this process than anyone. Whether it was wordsmithing, brainstorming about creative ways to present the information, or generating marketing ideas for the book, she's been there through it all. Soleil also read my first draft and provided helpful feedback that significantly improved the book. I can always rely on Soleil and hope that everyone has someone like her in their life.

My accountability partner, Dianne Morr who, among her many talents is a writing coach, provided me with a timeline for activities to ensure I got this book written and published by my deadline date. She provided ongoing support and, of course, accountability throughout the process. She also read my very first draft and provided some necessary edits.

I have been blessed with many colleagues and friends with different backgrounds and expertise who read the manuscript and provided input. I highly value each of their perspectives, experiences and wisdom. These colleagues include (in alphabetic order): Wendy Braun, Renee Hill, Toni

Marnul, Cyndi Maxey, Pam McElvane, Doug McKinley, Jackie Medland, Mark Sanborn, Ryan Schwartz, Donna St. Aubin and Lucy Zielinski. And thanks to Laura Nozicka who offered an array of creative and snappy book title options.

My editor, Tonie Harrington from Writing Connections who read through the manuscript with an objective and precise eye and found ways to tweak even the slightest details.

My book designer, Debbie Mackall at Shine Visual Communications, Inc. who expertly crafted the book's cover and laid out the internal pages to help communicate the message in a reader-friendly and creative manner.

And a very special "thank you" to Babs Brownyard who sadly passed away before seeing the final book in print. She challenged me to look at this project from a different perspective and helped me elevate the impact of the message as a result of her mastery, creativity and love. Her heart-print is on this book, and I know she would be proud with the end-result.

About the Author

Marcie Stern is a nationally known speaker, trainer and performance coach on the topics of leadership engagement, positive mindsets, and time and energy management. She is the founder and president of Marcie Stern & Associates, a professional development business and has worked with Fortune 500 companies, academic medical centers, and busy professionals to focus on what matters most. Marcie brings over two decades of progressive leadership, strategic planning and professional development experience with special expertise in the healthcare industry. She teaches the WAAMM™ principle (What Actions & Attitudes Matter Most) and "ENCORE" strategies that help clients get focused, engaged and in action on managing priorities, leveraging strengths, and accelerating goal achievement. Marcie is married to Scott and is the proud mother of her two sons, Matt and Nate. Together, they reside in a Chicago suburb.

www.marciestern.com

3620348R00060

Made in the USA
San Bernardino, CA
13 August 2013